Living *with* Grief and Loss

By Judy Murphy

PAAC Foundation   "Together we will build a better future."

The addition of this resource to the
John M. Cuelenaere Public Library
was made possible by the Prince Albert &
Area Community Foundation
2008 Literacy Grant.

OTS PRESS

berta

Living with Grief and Loss is published by
Grass Roots Press
A division of Literacy Services of Canada Ltd.
P.O. Box 52192, Edmonton, Alberta, T6G 2T5, Canada
Phone: 1-780-413-6491
Fax: 1-780-413-6582
Web: www.literacyservices.com

Author: Judy Murphy
Content consultation: Susan Patenaude, Tracy Duncan, Amy McLean, Cheryl Roberts
Editor: Pat Campbell
Copy editor: Graham Andrews
Consultant: Mary J. Breen
Illustrator: Val Lawton
Book design: Lara Minja, Lime Design Inc.
Printing: Imperial Printing, Edmonton

We acknowledge the financial support of the Government of Canada through the Book Publishing Industry Development Program (BPIDP) for our publishing activities.

We acknowledge the support of the Alberta Foundation for the Arts for our publishing programs.

We acknowledge funding from the Adult Learning, Literacy and Essential Skills Program, Human Resources and Social Development Canada.

Library and Archives Canada Cataloguing in Publication

Murphy, Judy, 1942–
        Living with grief and loss / Judy Murphy.

ISBN 1-894593-38-3

1. Readers for new literates. 2. Grief. 3. Caregivers. I. Title
I. Lawton, Valerie II. Title.

PE1126.N43M868 2006   428.6'2   C2006-9046646-6

Printed in Canada

Table of Contents

Thank You

Many people helped to put this book together.

Five focus groups were organized in Alberta to share ideas and knowledge about the content and appearance of the books in the Easy-to-Read Health Series. I wish to give special thanks to participants in Alberta's literacy and community programs.
Many people took part, and the following people gave permission to print their names:

Amanda Akkerman
Ann
Bill Littlejohn
C. Kameyosit
C. Monias
Darrell Demeria
Dave A. Ramsden
Debbie Longo
Della Akkerman
Delia Manychief
Denise Banack
Dione Dubois
Elvis Quintal
Ernie Lonewolf
Fred Cazon
Glen Dumon

Gloria Herbert
Hazel
Helen
Iwalani A. Post
Ive
Jeanne Longo
Jim Judd
John A. Butler
Jung Zheng
Kathy Helms
L. Miskenack
Lynne Gendron
Lynne W.
Liz
Mark Garbutt
Marvin Mochi
Matthew Ivan
Mavis Prevos
Monica Catellier
Nora Potts
Priscilla Wallin
Rachel Kretz
Robert Desjarlais
Shawn Worbs
Sherien Lo
Susan Murray
Terri Schneider
V. Faithful

I thank those who facilitated the focus groups and the programs and agencies who hosted them: Dani Ducross, Coordinator of Adult Literacy Program in Lacombe; Anna Reitman, Principal of Edmonton John Howard Society's Alternative Learning Program; Berniece Gowan and Sandra Loschnig, focus group facilitators at Calgary Elizabeth Fry Society; and Vesna Kavaz, Coordinator, Words Work in Athabasca.

People in the following organizations told me what information they would like to see in *Living with Grief and Loss*: Edmonton John Howard Society, Elizabeth Fry Society of Edmonton, and The Learning Centre Literacy Association.
I thank these people for their interest and for freely sharing their ideas.

Anna Holmes
April L. Williams
Austin Tootoosis
Barbara Lagrelle
Brenda Cardinal
Cindy L.
Darrell Demeria

Darrin Lamb
Dellia Halliday
Dianne B
Don Cooper
Donald Gouldhawke
Erin
G. BullChild
Jim Judd
John Butler
Jsunn
H.W.
Kamila Hofbauer
Marie Paquin
Mark Garbutt
Mary Ann Reo
Monica Dreaver
O.A.
Sandra Devries
Sean Beech
S.L.
Ryan Viznei
Tammy Toro
Tammy Wilson
Wendy Avery
W.L.C.

Participants in Edmonton John Howard's Alternative Learning Program, Elizabeth Fry Society of Edmonton, and The Learning Centre Literacy Association wrote stories about grief and loss in their lives. I thank Bev, Cindy Lingrell, G. BullChild, and Mary Ann Reo whose writings appear in this book.

The executive staff members at Boyle McCauley Health Centre, hosts of the Easy-to-Read Health Series project, have been enthusiastic and avid supporters. I thank Cecilia Blasetti, Colleen Novotny, and Wendy Kalamar.

The project has been guided by an Advisory Committee. Each member has given her time and knowledge to guide this project. I thank Marg Budd, Tobacco Reduction Consultant, Capital Health; Pat Campbell, President of Grass Roots Press; Ann Goldblatt, Project Evaluator; Jackie Norman, Coordinator of Changing Paths, Elizabeth Fry Society of Edmonton; and Colleen Novotny, Coordinator, Internal Operations, Boyle McCauley Health Centre.

I thank the project funder, Adult Learning, Literacy and Essential Skills Program, Human Resources and Social Development Canada, for its support. ●

Thank You!

Judy Murphy
Project Manager and Author
Easy-to-Read Health Series

(Welcome

During our lifetime, we all experience many kinds of losses. Some people lose their health. Others lose the jobs they need to feed their families. And most of us lose some people we love. Grief is a normal reaction to any kind of loss. The ideas in this book will help you deal with loss and grief. You will also learn how to help children deal with loss and death.

This book focuses on the loss of a loved one. It also gives you ideas about how to care for a person who is dying. The ideas in this book will also help you care for yourself.

In this book, we talk about death as part of a journey. There are lots of choices to make on this journey. This book will help you prepare for the death of a loved one and for your own death.

♣ food for thought

And now the end is near
And so I face the final curtain,
My friends, I'll say it clear,
I'll state my case of which I'm certain.
I've lived a life that's full,
I've travelled each and evr'y highway
And more, much more than this,
I did it my way.

— Paul Anka

(1 Grieving

During our life time, we experience many losses. Some losses are very big, like the death of someone we love. Smaller losses, like losing a favourite jacket, don't affect us so much.

Types of losses

- Friends who die, move away or no longer want to be friends
- Relatives who die or move away
- Pets who die or are lost
- Loss of hearing, eyesight, a limb or the ability to walk easily
- A miscarriage or an abortion
- Being unable to reach a dream
- Not marrying the one we love

What are my experiences with grief and loss?

> My friends are grieving for their son's death

> Accidental death

> Suicide of a friend

> Death of an uncle and other family because of addictions

> As you get older you can't do things for yourself

> Younger deaths around crime, drugs, addictions, gang activity

— Participants in the Alternative Learning Program, Edmonton John Howard Society

- A child taken by child welfare
- A job loss
- Loss of freedom because of being sent to prison

Grief

Grief is the natural reaction to loss.

The word, *grief*, comes from a French word that means heavy. Grief can feel like it is weighing us down.

Grief is natural, but people go through grief in many different ways. How we grieve depends on things such as our culture, our age, and how much support we have from our family and friends. Quite often, we grieve in the same way that people in our families do.

It's important to remember that grief affects your *whole* person. It affects your emotions, your body, your spirit, and your mind.

Grief Affects the Whole Person

How your mind can be affected by loss

- You deny that it has happened.
- It's hard to think clearly.
- Small problems seem big.
- Your loss is the only thing you think about.
- You are not interested in other people.
- You keep asking yourself: "Why did this happen?"

How your emotions can be affected by loss

- sadness
- feeling all alone
- guilt
- anger
- fear
- depression
- sometimes, relief that it's over

How your body can be affected by loss

- numbness
- shortness of breath
- a heavy feeling in your chest
- tired all the time
- sleeping problems
- headaches
- hair loss

How your spirit can be affected by loss

- Blaming yourself or the person who has died
- Feeling that there is no meaning to life
- Wanting to die
- Not feeling connected to your own spirit
- Thinking a lot about the afterlife

♣ **food for thought**

...life and death are one, even as the river and the sea are one.

— Kahlil Gibran

Grieving can be a lonely journey. We all have to take this journey in order to heal, but we don't need to do it alone. Try to find some people who will let you talk about your grief. You could also go to a therapist or a health worker if you feel you need more help.

Your Losses

Take a few minutes to think of a loss you have had in the last year. Close your eyes and try to remember how you felt. Think about how this loss affected your body, your mind, your emotions, and your spirit.

I am sorry my birth children did not live. I tried three times....First there was a miscarriage. Then I had five-and-a-half month pregnancies. The babies had just started to move and kick. I miscarried. My then husband only allowed me a short grieving period. Eventually, I came to realize I could not have children biologically. I came to accept adoption and I have three children — Andy, Jeff, and Tami.

— Cindy Lingrell

Type of Loss	How did you respond?
○ My favourite aunt died.	○ I couldn't sleep or eat.
_____	_____
_____	_____
_____	_____
_____	_____

Stages of Grief

Marie learned that she had a type of cancer that would spread very quickly. She only had four months to live. She had many different feelings before she was able to accept the truth. Then she was able to prepare for her death.

When Mark returned home from his upgrading program, he learned that his dog had been killed by a car. Right away, he took a bus to the vet's clinic. He wanted to see the dog and say goodbye. Mark moved back and forth between feeling angry, guilty, and depressed in a very short time. After a few months, he was able to look ahead and think about getting another dog.

Moving through the stages of grief

Marie and Mark had different kinds of losses, and they felt their grief in different ways.

People who study grief say there are different stages of grief. Although we each go through these stages when we have a loss, we make this journey in different ways. Some of us go through each stage one after another. Others might move back and forth between the stages. People also stay in each stage for different lengths of time.

Shock and Denial

In the first stage, people often deny the loss. They might say, "This is not true. My child is not dead." They often feel shocked and numb, as if nothing is real.

Anger

People often feel angry. They might be angry at the person who delivered the bad news to them. They might also be angry at the person who is dying or has died, or the pet that ran away. If there is someone to blame, such as the driver of the car that killed their pet, then they might be very angry at that person.

Guilt

People often feel guilty about something they've said or done. For example, they might feel terrible that the last time they saw their brother, they had a big argument, and they didn't have time to patch it up.

Depression

After people understand that their loss is real and lasting, people usually feel a very deep sadness. This sadness might feel like it will never end.

Acceptance

After awhile, people begin to see that the loss will always be part of them. They accept that they will still miss the person who has died, and they can still love the person. Gradually, they begin to see that they will have to go on living in a different way without the person they loved.

Growth

The last stage is growth. This is the stage when people begin to move forward with their lives. This is when they begin to plan for a new life. Some people reach this stage within weeks. For others, it takes years.

Remember: people who are dying also go through these stages as they grieve the ending of their lives.

♣ **food for thought**

You can clutch the past so tightly to your chest that it leaves your arms too full to embrace the present.

— Jan Glidewell

Depression

✤ food for thought

Take your own time, but be sure to walk over the ground again. You must do so because whatever you run away from runs you.

— Gay Hendricks

Some people who are sad for a very long time become depressed. Here are some signs that you may be depressed. Check the ones that describe you. Think about the past two months.

If you feel one or more of these things, you may be depressed. Go and talk to a counsellor, rabbi, iman, minister, or elder. You really can get help, and you will feel better.

Signs of depression

- ○ I feel tired all the time.
- ○ I feel empty and worthless.
- ○ I feel helpless.
- ○ I don't feel like eating.
- ○ I have trouble getting anything done.

- ○ I have trouble sleeping.
- ○ I've stopped doing the things I used to like.
- ○ I've stopped seeing my friends or my family.
- ○ I've been thinking about suicide.

Dealing with loss

Some people keep all their feelings to themselves because they think crying is a sign of weakness. Others don't show their feelings because they don't want to bother people with their problems.

This is usually a mistake. Grieving is natural and human, and we need to feel all the feelings that come up. Keeping them bottled-up inside doesn't help. It stops us from working through our grief.

> Cry. Cry. Cry. You miss your family or good friends. Sometimes it is hard to cry but it makes our spirit let go.
>
> — G. BullChild

Have you lost a loved one? How did you deal with your loss? Did you...

- ○ Talk about your feelings?
- ○ Write about your feelings?
- ○ Join a support group?
- ○ Make time to be alone?
- ○ Ask for counselling?

Were there other things that you did that were helpful?

_____

_____

_____

♣ food for thought

Let your journey be what it is.
And let yourself…be who you are.

— Alan D. Wolfelt

If you are feeling grief, talk about your loss to someone who will listen—a friend or a counsellor. Talk and talk until your words run out. When your mind fills up with words and thoughts again, start talking again. Talking to others can make you feel less alone. Talking can help you make sense of your loss.

Our minds are like tape recorders: they can play the same words over and over again. You might find that some thoughts keep repeating themselves in your head. "If only I hadn't gone out that day," or, "If only I'd been at home when the police called." When *"If only…"* keeps playing in your head, you probably want to stop hearing the words. Try taking a fast walk or bike ride. This will help to turn off the tape recorder in your mind. Without these messages playing in your head, you will have more energy to carry on.

Even though your grief might be making you tired, try some new activities. Perhaps you will meet some new people. And, being active actually helps your body release some of the pain of your loss.

Most people in our society don't cry very easily, especially men. Many people believe that strong people never cry. People who are really sad are often afraid that once they start crying, they will never stop. Try to let your tears flow. Crying is nature's way of cleansing our bodies to let go of our tension and stress. Even crying a little bit at a time is helpful.

Some people take sedatives to dull their emotions. These can help in the first few days after a death; however, it's not a good idea to take them for a long time. You need to feel your grief with your whole body and all your senses. Sedatives, like tranquillizers and alcohol, make this harder to do.

Pay attention to your body's needs as you grieve. If you are tired, then get extra sleep. And don't forget to eat well. Comfort foods—foods that bring back good memories, such as bannock or hot chocolate—might make you feel better.

❖ food for thought

Grief is itself a medicine.

— William Cowp

A few weeks after my brother died, while I was grieving, I was lying in the same spot we had prayed together before, and I felt him embrace me and felt him say, "Thank you." I will always treasure those seconds or minutes of that feeling. The worst part of my grieving was over. I knew he was OK, and so was I.

– Bev

Create some rituals that keep alive your memories of the person you have lost. Pick something that has a special meaning for you. You can do these rituals alone or with someone else. Here are some rituals others have done:

- Light a special candle.

- Put fresh wildflowers in a vase.

- Read a poem you love each night before going to bed.

Make time to connect with your spirit in ways that matter to you. Get closer to nature by going for a walk, or visit a church, temple or mosque. You can also write in your journal or meditate.

Remember: time is the best healer of all. And, time works best if you allow yourself to feel your emotions. As time goes on, you will slowly begin to feel better. Grieving is never quick and easy.

Supporting a grieving person

Here are some ways to support a grieving person.

Be a good friend. Sit with your friend and let them express their feelings—their anger, their sadness, and perhaps their guilt. You don't have to say anything. Your quiet support is enough. Let the person know that you are with them on their journey. Let them know they are not alone.

Remember: this can take a long time. Grieving doesn't follow a clock or schedule. It is different for everyone.

Accept. Listen to and accept your friend's words. It is not helpful to say, "I know how you feel" or "It was for the best." These words will not lessen your friend's pain. Just listen.

Help. Give your friend a hand with day-to-day tasks such as shopping for food, cleaning, laundry or taking the kids to school or daycare. Look

❖ food for thought

We are each of us angels with only one wing, and we can only fly by embracing one another.

— Luciano de Crescenzo

I have witnessed three deaths in my lifetime in my family. My grandmother was crippled up and bed-ridden by being paralyzed. I was very young at the time. It was very hard for me to see her being in that stage. That was in Europe.

Both my mother and my husband knew they were dying.... [I] felt sorrow, turmoil, and helpless not being able to help them. There [was] also anger, uncertainty, a lot of crying on all parties involved.

Even to this day, I am trying to cope with my loss and loneliness and closeness I have shared with the three people I loved the most.

I mainly regret not being able to say goodbye to them and help them.

— Mary Ann Reo

around for what needs to be done and offer to help. Just saying, "Call me if you need anything" is not enough. People who are upset don't think clearly, so they probably can't give you a list of how you could help. Make some offers.

Listen. Your friend will need to make decisions. You can help by getting the person to talk through what needs to be done. Talking out loud helps us think more clearly. You do not have to have the answers. You just need open ears and an open heart.

Take care of yourself. When you help someone who is grieving, it is OK to put limits on what you can offer. You still need to take care of your own needs. Take time to eat well, get enough sleep and do something fun or relaxing.

Everyone reacts to losses in different ways. When you are grieving, be gentle with yourself. Accept what you are feeling and don't judge it. Feeling grief is normal, but grieving is one of the hardest things to experience.

And if you would like some help, ask for it. You do not need to make this journey alone. •

✤ food for thought

Hope is grief's best music.

— unknown

(2 Helping Children Grieve

How Children Feel

Denise is eight years old. Denise's father abused her mother.
One day, Denise's mother left her father. She took Denise and
her younger brother to a women's shelter. Denise feels lost
and confused. She is also very sad about leaving her home,
her father, and her friends.

Jamal is 10 years old. He got a dog named Lucky for his sixth
birthday. The two were always together. Then Jamal's father
lost his job, and the family had to move to an apartment.
No pets are allowed in the apartment, so Jamal has to find a
new home for Lucky. His father cannot understand why Jamal
is upset about saying goodbye to his dog. The father keeps
saying, "It's just a dog. Get over it. Big boys don't cry."

❖ food for thought
Even in the wilderness,
stars can still shine.

— Aoi Jiyuu Shiroi Nozomi

Glen was 13 years old when his grandfather died. Glen was very close to his grandfather. They spent a lot of time together. His grandfather taught Glen how to fish, hunt, and carve wooden animals. When his grandfather was dying in a nursing home, Glen's mother always took Glen with her to visit. She talked to Glen about death and how it is part of life's natural cycle. She always tried to be honest about what was happening. She answered Glen's questions as best she could.

♣ **food for thought**

"I'll cry with you,"

she whispered

"until we run out of tears.

Even if it's forever.

We'll do it together."

— Molly Fumia

Children experience many kinds of loss. Some children lose people in their families. Others lose pets they love. Others lose friends when they move or go to a new school. When children's parents divorce, the children lose their day-to-day routines.

Children feel grief just as much as adults do, but they show their grief differently. By understanding how children grieve, we can help them better.

Signs of Grief

Here are some ways children show that they are grieving.

- They show strong feelings such as anger.
- They seem confused.
- They become uninterested in things they used to like.
- They get into trouble at school.

♣ food for thought
Remember sadness is always
temporary. It too shall pass.

— Chuck T. Falcon

- They have problems sleeping.
- They have nightmares.
- They are afraid of being alone.
- They don't want to be with their friends.
- They act younger than they are. They might wet the bed, or start sucking their thumb.
- They talk about suicide.

When children talk about things they have lost, listen and answer as best you can.

Remember: if you don't know the answer, simply say, "I don't know." Also remember that children often ask the same question over and over again.

The next page lists some questions children often ask. In the blank space, write your answers to the questions. Then, read how others might answer the question.

What should I say?

Questions children ask[2]	What would you say?	Ideas for answering
What is a funeral?		A funeral is a way for us to say goodbye to someone we love. It is a time for everyone to share their feelings.
Where do dead people go?		When a person dies, their body stops living. Many people believe that a part of the person lives on in our hearts and memories. This part is called a soul or spirit.
Why do people die?		There are lots of reasons. Sometimes people get very sick or have an accident that makes their body stop working. Sometimes people grow old and die just like trees, plants, and animals do.
Will I die, too?		Everyone will die one day. Usually children are strong and healthy, and live long lives.
Will you die?		All people die. You will always have people to love and care for you.

What should I say? *continued...*

Questions children ask[2]	What would you say?	Ideas for answering
Why do I feel scared?		All your feelings are OK. Feeling sad, angry, scared, and lonely are normal. Sometimes you will feel these things a lot, and other times not so much.
What can I do when I feel really bad?		When we feel very sad or angry, it is scary. Share your feelings with a grownup that you feel safe with. Talking about how we feel makes us feel better.
What is death?		Death means that someone or something is no longer living. Death is forever. It is not like sleeping a long time. When someone dies, they don't come back.
Why did someone I love have to die?		This is very hard to understand. Everyone feels very sad when we lose someone we love. Death is part of nature, just like birth.

How can we help children grieve?

Children need to learn about death. If the dying person is at home, children can be part of taking care of the person. If the person is in the hospital, include the child as much as possible. You can begin talking about the life cycle at any time. Children often ask questions about animals, bugs, pets, and plants, so use examples from nature when you talk about dying.

Here are some ways to help kids handle their grief.

Listen

- Encourage children to talk about their feelings.

- Grieving can take a long time. Listen to the child talk about the death, no matter how long it takes.

- Children may feel sad again on the loved one's birthday or the anniversary of death. Make time to listen.

Talk

- Tell them over and over that they are loved.

- Make sure they understand that getting sick doesn't always mean someone will die.

- Tell them that it's OK to cry.

- Tell them that they are safe, and that they will always be cared for.

- Answer their questions honestly and simply.

Do

- Help them to share their feelings in different ways. They can draw, paint, tell a story, dance, make things or play with puppets.

- Spend time with your children.

- Try to keep the day-to-day routine the same as it was before the loss. Children will feel more secure if their routine is as normal as possible.

- Ask if they would like a photograph of the person they loved or something special that belonged to them. Let them choose one they like.

- Make a scrapbook with the child about the person or pet who has died. Ask the child to tell you stories about the person or pet. Write them down and put them in the scrapbook.

Do not stand at my grave and weep[3]

Do not stand at my grave and weep,
I am not there, I do not sleep.

I am a thousand winds that blow.
I am the diamond glint on snow.
I am the sunlight on ripened grain.
I am the gentle autumn rain.

When you wake in the morning hush,
I am the swift, uplifting rush
Of quiet birds in circling flight.
I am the soft starlight at night.

Do not stand at my grave and weep.
I am not there, I do not sleep.
Do not stand at my grave and cry.
I am not there, I did not die.

— Mary Frye

Helping children deal with grief may not be easy, but it is one of the most important things an adult can do. If you can help children learn about managing grief when they are young, you will be giving them skills they can use when they are older. •

❖ **food for thought**

Walk on a rainbow trail; walk
on a trail of song, and all about
you will be beauty. There is a
way out of every dark mist,
over a rainbow trail.

— Navajo Song

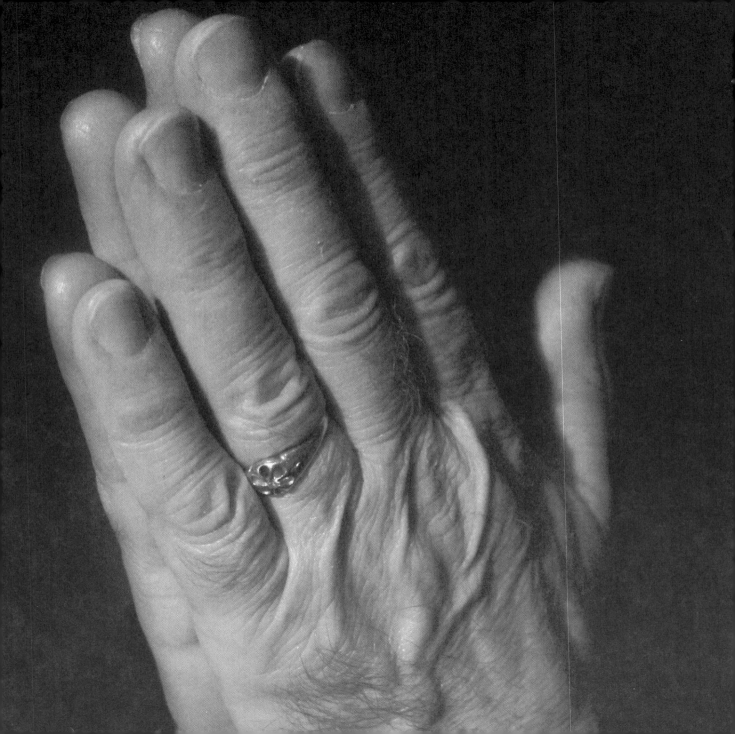

(3 Giving Care

Anita visits her 88-year-old mother every day. Her mother has lived a long and full life. Now she lives in a nursing home in a big city, and many nurses and doctors look after her needs.

Arnold and Darrell are best friends. Darrell lives with Arnold on the reserve. Darrell has AIDS and is close to death. Arnold has taken time off work to care for his friend full-time. The Elder visits every day. Other people bring food and stay with Darrell. This extra help allows Arnold to have some time to himself.

Tim and Fred are cousins. They were driving home after working a long shift when Fred fell asleep at the wheel. The car went off the road and rolled several times. Tim wasn't wearing his seat belt, and he was thrown from the car. Tim had a very serious head injury. The ambulance took him to the hospital and the doctors put him on life-support. Tim will die without it. Now his parents have to decide how long Tim should stay on life-support.

❖ **food for thought**
The most important thing I know now [about dying people] that I didn't know then is this: People who are dying are still living."

— David Kuhl

♣ **food for thought**

There is nothing more beautiful
than an...old face with the
lines that tell a story, a story
of a life that has been lived
with some fullness.

— Helen Hayes

Dying is a journey. Each of these people is on a
different journey. Each person is moving toward
death in a different way.

One day, you might need to care for a dying relative, partner, or friend. Perhaps you'll be looking after the person at home, or perhaps you'll be supporting them in the hospital. This chapter talks about how to care for someone who is dying.

Caring for someone who is near death

Near death, you will see many changes. These changes affect the person's body, mind, emotions, and spirit. In other words, the *whole* person is affected. Keep this in mind so you can give support and care to the whole person, not just the body.

Talking and Listening

You are probably wondering what you should say to a dying person. You do not have to say anything. You can keep them company. Simply sit beside the person and hold their hand.

If the person feels like talking, you can listen. Sometimes, a dying person will say something that makes you feel uncomfortable. For example, the person might say, "I'm tired of fighting. I just want to die." It is not a good idea to say, "Don't talk that way." In other words, accept what you hear, and try not to judge.

The person might want to talk about dying. If so, ask, "What are you thinking? How do you feel?" It might be hard to listen to someone talk about dying, but try. A good listener can make the dying person feel calm and safe.

The person who is dying might want to talk about their life and what they have learned. Encourage them to share their life stories. If they are well enough to answer questions, ask how they felt about certain events. Ask questions about their youth and their parents and grandparents. If you have a tape recorder, ask if you can record these stories. In later years, these stories will provide you with special memories.

The person who is dying might be very quiet. If they want to be quiet, then respect this. Some dying people are too short of breath to talk. If they seem interested, you could tell them stories about themselves and some people they know. Remember that dying people can usually still hear. Many people forget this and talk as if the person cannot hear or understand.

If you have to make decisions that will affect the dying person, you may need to ask them some questions.

Common Fears

Dying people are often afraid. Some people talk about their fears, and others don't. Talking helps, so let the person know that you are willing to listen if they want to talk about what they are afraid of.

Will I feel pain?

How will I *die*?

Am I being a burden?

Common fears of dying people:

- "Will I have a lot of pain?"

- "Am I a burden?"

- "Will I lose control of my body?"

- "Do you think my family will respect my wishes after I die?"

- "What will happen to me after death?"

♣ **food for thought**

Let not your heart be weary, neither let it be afraid.

— John 14:27

People are often afraid of dying alone. To prevent this from happening, find out which people they would like around them, and invite these people to visit around the clock. Also, ask if she wants an elder, pastor, imam, or rabbi. This way, the person will not die alone.

Signs that death is near

Needs

The dying person might not know how to ask for help, especially if they are afraid of being a burden. So, find out as much as you can about what they need. Let the person know that you want to help. For example, find out if they need more pain killers.

Ways to help people feel more comfortable:

- relaxing music

- soft lights

- a change of positions

- calm, quiet talking

- a wipe of the face and neck with a soft damp cloth

Even when people are dying, they like to feel they can still be useful to others. For example, your mother might tell you that she does not need anything right away. She is thinking of you so that you can have a rest

♣ food for thought

I need someone who believes
that the sun will rise again, but
who does not fear my darkness,
someone who can point out
the rocks in my way without
making me a child by carrying
me, someone who can stand
in thunder and watch the
lightning and believe in a
rainbow.

— Fr. Joe Mahoney

or do things you want to do. Respect her need to help you even if it is in a small way.

Some dying people need permission to die. Without it, they might fight to stay alive, and then have more pain and suffering. If you think this is happening, tell them, "If you are ready to die, it is OK."

Confusion

Dying people are often confused about day-to-day things. They forget where they are or what day it is, and who people are. If this happens, listen to what the person is saying and gently remind them of peoples' names or what day it is. Dying people can also be confused about who is alive and who is dead. For example, they might think they saw their mother last night. Even though you know their mother is dead, the person might get comfort from talking to a loved one who has died. Listen and accept what the person is saying.

Daily routines help people who are confused. For example, you could begin some visits by brushing your friend's hair and end the visits by looking at photos.

Breathing

Just before death, the person's breathing will change. The breath becomes uneven. It may speed up or slow down. Sometimes they won't breathe at all for a minute or more. The person might moan and you might hear a gurgling or rattling sound. These sounds may frighten you, but they do not mean that the person is uncomfortable.

A change of position can help. Try putting pillows under the person's head and upper back, or turn them gently onto one side and put pillows against their back. A fan or a humidifier in the room can also help to ease the breathing.

Blood Flow

When a person is dying, their blood flows more slowly. The skin becomes colder and darker. If you notice that their skin feels

✤ **food for thought**
Wherever there is a human being, there is an opportunity for kindness.

— Seneca

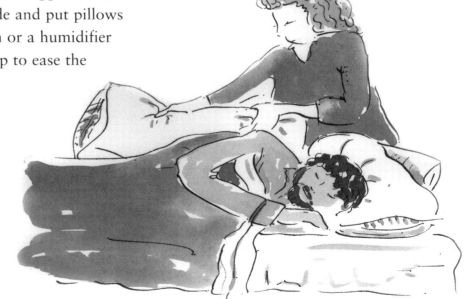

cold, ask if they want more covers. A gentle massage on the forehead, hands, and feet can also help.

Eating and Drinking

♣ **food for thought**

Death is as natural as life, and should be sweet and graceful.

— Raph Waldo Emerson

Dying people lose their appetite. They eat and drink less and less. Just offer small servings of their favourite foods. Make sure they are soft so they are easy to swallow.

If the person is not drinking, their throat and lips will become dry. You can offer them ice chips, small sips of water, or wet their lips with a soft damp cloth. If the person stops eating and drinking entirely, they will produce much less urine. It will be a darker colour and it will smell stronger.

The dying person might lose control of their bowels and bladder, and this might be embarrassing. Let them know that this is normal. Ask if it is OK to change the sheets so that the bed is fresh and clean.

It is very painful when someone close to us dies. It is hard to know what has to be done right away. The next chapter, *Making Arrangements*, will help you. •

$\big(4$ Making Arrangements

Juanita died at home after a long illness. Juanita's son, daughter, and father were with her when she died. Juanita had written notes about the kind of service she wanted when she died. She had also talked about her wishes with her family and friends. She knew that she wanted everyone to celebrate her life.

Eli was riding his motorcycle home after visiting his girlfriend. It was a dark and rainy night. A truck driver didn't see Eli turn the corner in front of him. The truck driver drove right into Eli. Even though he was taken to the hospital, Eli died later that night. The hospital phoned his parents to tell them that Eli was dead.

Some people plan ahead and take care of their affairs. Others might think that death is far in the future and there will be lots of time to plan later. People close to a person who has died find it easier to cope when they know how the person would like to be remembered.

❧ food for thought

What we call the beginning is often the end. To make an end is to make a beginning. The end is where we start from.

— T.S. Eliot

Making arrangements for the person's body

In addition to your grief, there are things that have to be done soon after the death. The steps listed here are for those who are close to the person who has died.

1. Family and close friends might want to spend time with the body of the person who has died so they can say their final goodbyes. They might want to touch the body one last time and they might want to pray. It is important to give people time to do this.

2. If the person has died in the hospital, the hospital might let you see the body one more time. You might also have to go to the hospital to pick up their personal things.

3. You need to arrange for a place to send the body. If the person dies in the hospital and you want the body to go to a funeral home, the hospital staff will help you. If the death is expected and happens at home, you can call the funeral home. If the death is not expected, you might want to call the person's doctor, the hospital or the police to get information on what to do next.

Even animals grieve. Patsy, a 40-year-old elephant died in the Toronto Zoo. The zookeepers left the elephant's body in with the other six elephants she had lived with so that they could say goodbye. These six elephants stayed with her through the night. They brushed her with their trunks and seemed to be grieving for their friend.

4. Paperwork will need to be done to take care of financial and legal affairs. You might need a death certificate or a certificate of burial. The funeral home can help get the paperwork you need.

   You can ask for extra official copies of the death certificate or certificate of burial. You can get these from the funeral director, or from a city or county office. You will need these later when you look after the financial and legal details.

❖ **food for thought**

Death is not putting out the light. It is only extinguishing a lamp because the day has come.

— Rabindranath Tagore

5. You will probably want to let people know about the death. If you don't want to make these calls, ask a close friend or relative to call for you. You could also ask a priest, minister, pastor, imam, rabbi or elder. If you have to make these calls yourself, you might want a counsellor or a close friend to be with you.

Tip: If you know that someone is dying, it's a good idea to have all the names and phone numbers ahead of time.

It is hard to think of all the people to call when someone has just died and you are upset.

6. Find out if the person has plans for their funeral and burial.

Planning the service

A funeral or memorial service is a way to honour the person who has died.

A funeral service can be very helpful for those who are left behind.

- It helps people heal.
- It helps people accept the death.
- It brings friends and family together.
- It make a place for people to support each other.
- It gives people a chance to share their feelings.
- It lets people tell stories about the dead person and this helps builds memories.

There are many ways to show your love and respect for someone who has died. Each culture has special traditions for funerals. What types of services have you gone to? How was the person honoured?

A **traditional funeral service** takes place in a church or funeral home. Sometimes, this is followed by a burial.

A **memorial service** can be held anywhere, and at any time. A memorial service is sometimes held when a person is being cremated.

❧ **food for thought**

Death leaves a heartache no one can heal, love leaves a memory no one can steal.

— from a headstone in Ireland

Some decisions to make:

- Did the person leave directions about the service they wanted?
- Did they want to be buried or cremated?
- Did they want to be buried in a casket?
- If they wanted to be cremated, did they ask for their ashes to be buried, scattered, or kept in an urn?

If you don't know what the person wanted, you will have to make those decisions yourself. Try to think about the type of service the person would want. These are hard choices, but many people find it comforting to plan something special for the person they loved.

My family are Mennonite farmers. Whenever I visit anyone in my family for dinner or just coffee, one of the first things the women do is pull out the photo albums. In them there are pictures of the living and the dead in their coffins — even babies. They talk about them the same way they talk about the living.

— Writer at Elizabeth Fry Society of Edmonton

What traditions does your family follow when a relative has died?

_____

_____

_____

_____

Costs of funerals and memorial services

Services can cost a lot. Call a local funeral home.
Ask about the choices and how much each will cost.

Funerals are expensive. Here are some of the costs:

- Preparation of the body
- Purchase of the casket
- Use of a room for visitation and/or for a ceremony
- Use of cars to go from the funeral home or church to the grave yard
- The burial or cremation

If a funeral is too expensive, you could apply for public aid or social assistance. You can also ask a funeral director for this information.

A notice in the paper

You might want to put a notice in the paper to let others know about the person's death. The

♣ food for thought
I cannot think of death
as more than the going out
of one room into another.

—William Blake

death notice or obituary gives details about the service and about the person. Ask someone who knew the person well to write the notice.

Check on costs. Some newspapers charge for each line or word. Find out when you need to send it to the paper to have it printed in time. ●

Writing an obituary

Some things you might want to include in the obituary	Example
The person's full name Put nicknames in quotes.	David Paul "Rocket" Duchene
Age	28 years of age
Date and place of death	July 15, 2006 in Saskatoon
Reason for death	He died in a car accident.
Where he was born and what job he did	He was born in Regina. He was finishing Grade 11 at the Community College.
Clubs and church he belonged to	He was a member of the karate club and coached seven and eight year olds.
Hobbies and interests he had	He loved singing and playing guitar in the band, Mountain Creek Boys.
Any awards or achievements he had	He won first place in the regional karate competition last year.
Any of his family members who died before him	His parents, Marie and Jim Duchene, and younger brother, Dan, died five years ago in a car accident.
Members of his close family who are living	He left behind his common-law wife, Anne, and his two children, Frankie, age two and Billy, age four, as well as his sister, Louise, and brother, Paul.

Writing an obituary continued...

Some things you might want to include in the obituary	Example
Something about him that you want others to remember	Rocket made people laugh when the times were hard. He was always there for his friends and was a good listener.
Name of the funeral home and place, date, and time of the service	A memorial service to honour his life will be held at the home of the deceased, 1234 St. Anthony Street, Saskatoon on July 18, 2006 at 2 p.m.

In Loving Memory

❧ **food for thought**

Death is the end of a stage,
not the end of the journey.

— Sir Oliver Lodge

(5 Caring for Yourself

Jamal is taking holiday time from work so that he can look after his mother who is dying at home. He has called some of his mother's friends, her neighbours, and his cousins to ask for their help. Jamal showed them a list of things he needs help with, and asked them what they would like do. He also asked them when they would be free to come by to help. He made a weekly schedule that shows who is doing what and when, and he gave a copy to each person. Jamal's mother likes to have her friends nearby and the friends, neighbours, and cousins feel good about being able to help. Jamal makes sure he still gets to the gym for a workout three times a week, and he meets his girlfriend for coffee on Saturday mornings.

Ana's younger sister, Leila, died of cancer last year. Ana quit her job so that she could spend time with Leila in the hospital. Ana slept on a chair that made into a small bed in Leila's room so that she didn't have to leave her. She spent all

❖ **food for thought**
There's no better way to energize your body, mind, and spirit than by taking care of yourself.

— Stephanie Tourles

her time at the hospital where she read to Leila and tried to make her more comfortable. Lots of friends and family members offered to come and stay with Leila, but Ana said, "No, thank you. I can do it."

You are giving someone a very special gift when you support them while they are dying. You can make a big difference in their life.

Looking after someone who is dying is not an easy job. Even though you might feel good about being able to do this, it can still make you tired and stressed. This is a time when you also need to look after yourself. This is not being selfish. If you don't look after yourself, you won't be able to look after anyone else. You won't have enough energy, and the dying person might end up worrying about *you*.

Here are some things you can do to stay well while you are looking after someone who is dying.

Ask for help

Keep in touch with your friends and family and ask them to help you. Most people want to help in some way. People find it easier to help if they know which jobs need to be done. Don't be shy to say what kind of help you need.

Here are some things you can ask others to do:

- Clean or tidy your home

- Go for a walk with you

- Keep you company

- Watch TV with you

- Help prepare your meals

A schedule for your family and friends can be very helpful. Here is a schedule that Maureen made for her friends while she was looking after her brother, Fred.

♣ **food for thought**

May the gentleness of spring rains
soften the tensions within us,
And the power of ocean waves
steady and strengthen us.

— Janet Schaffran and Pat Kozak

Schedule

Name of friend	Mon	Tue	Wed	Thurs	Fri	Sat	Sun
Valerie	Clean the kitchen			Laundry			
Mark						Buy groceries	
Jose		Stay with Fred while I go for a walk				Stay with Fred while I go for a walk		
Helen		Go for a walk with me				Go for a walk with me		Stay with with Fred so I can make some phone calls
Maria			Cook and visit with me				

Learn to say "No."

It takes lots of time and energy to care for a dying person, and your family might not understand how little time you have for them. You're going to have to learn to say "No" when others ask you for favours. Some people have to practise saying "No, thank you!" If you find it hard to say "No," say, "I'll need time to think about that." Then come back later and say, "No, I'm not able to help you at this time."

♣ food for thought

Keep your face to the sunshine and you cannot see the shadow. It's what sunflowers do.

— Helen Keller

Take care of yourself

You need your strength at this time, so be sure to eat well. Don't skip meals because you are too busy. Try to eat good food, and get lots of sleep. A little exercise every day can make you feel much better.

Lift your spirits

Make time to be alone. Choose things that calm you and make you happy. Some people write or draw in a journal, others play with a dog. Others sit with a book and a cup of tea.

Calm your mind and body

Learn some ways to release your stress. Then you won't get so tired that you end up sick too. Talk with friends about how you feel. Try taking a walk outdoors or take long baths or regular naps.

Some people use deep breathing to release their stress. One way to feel calmer is to notice your breath as it moves in and out of your body. Do not try to change anything. Just focus on your breath, breathing in and breathing out for a few minutes. When you focus on your breath, your mind becomes more quiet and still.

Try this breathing exercise if you feel stressed or worried. It only takes a few minutes to do.

STEP 1: Sit comfortably in a chair. Close your eyes or look gently toward your heart.

STEP 2: Try to hold your back straight and tall but also relaxed.

STEP 3: Pay attention as you breathe in and breathe out. Just follow your breath for a few breaths.

STEP 4: Without forcing or changing your breath, count one, two as you breathe in, smoothly and easily. Hold your breath as you count one, two. Then breathe out for two counts. Pause for two counts. Keep repeating the pattern for a few minutes.

STEP 5: Then breathe normally again. Notice if you feel calmer and more relaxed.

Can you pick two ideas that you might try to give you some support? Can you think of any more ideas? An example will help start you off.

Topics	My idea	My support
Ask for help.	I am going to take a 20-minute walk every day after supper.	My brother will stay with my mother so I can go for a walk.
Learn to say "No."		

Topics	My idea	My support
Take care of yourself		
Lift your spirits		
Calm your mind and body		

These are good ways to take care of yourself anytime. You don't have to wait until you are caring for someone who is dying.

Remember: make time to look after yourself—even if it is just ten minutes sitting quietly on a balcony or on a doorstep watching the sun set or listening to music. Even though you may think this is not the time to treat yourself, do it. It's good for your own well-being and for those you want to look after. ●

♣ food for thought

The journey begins right here. In the middle of the road. Right beneath your feet. This is the place. There is no other place. There is no other time.

— David Whyte

(6 Getting Ready for Your Journey

After a long struggle with diabetes, Darren died of a heart attack. He was only 40 years old. He was a hard worker and he was good at saving money for the future. He had paid off the mortgage on the home he shared with his common-law wife and their two children. His roots to his First Nations' community were strong. Darren's family knew exactly how he wanted things handled after his death.

Sadie was 66 when she died at home. She lived in her apartment with her two cats. The day before she died, she had tea with her friend and did her grocery shopping that afternoon. She felt a little tired when she got home, so she took a nap. She died in her sleep. Sadie had two married sons in their early 40s. She had never gotten around to writing a will. When she had tried to talk with her sons about her death, they always changed the subject. No one knew what she wanted for a service.

❖ food for thought

Let your journey be what it is.

And let yourself...be who you are.

— Alan D. Wolfelt

Whatever your age—18 or 99—it's a good idea to think about what will happen when you die. Who will look after your family? What will happen to your things? Death seems far away when we are young, but a plan for what happens when you die can be very helpful.

This chapter is for those who want to get ready for their death.

Lots of decisions to make

Many people find it hard to make decisions about their own death. Family members are often no help as they don't want to think about it either. Even so, it's important to talk about these things with the people you care about.

You probably care a lot about what happens to your children, your family, and your things. You can help your family and friends by writing down what you want to happen. Then, after you die, they will know what you want and they can carry out your wishes.

Wills

There are three kinds of wills:

- Legal wills

- Living wills

- Spiritual wills

♣ **food for thought**

No one can really stop growing old...Since there is no use fighting against nature one might just as well end with a grand finale of peace and serenity and spiritual contentment and not with the crash of a broken drum or cracked cymbals.

— Lin Yutang

Legal Will

Darren made a legal will as soon as his first child was born. He changed his will after his second and third children were born. He and his wife have talked about what will happen to their children if they both die before the children are grown up. They want Darren's brother to raise their children, so Darren asked his brother if that was OK. When he agreed, Darren named him as the children's guardian. Darren also made a list of who will get their things. Darren and his wife asked her sister to be the executor of the will to make sure their wishes are followed.

Sadie didn't have a will. After she died, Sadie's friends and family had different ideas about what she wanted. Her sons argued over who will have her things, including her house. Her best friend, Maria, knew that Sadie wanted her older son to have the house, but the younger son didn't believe Maria. Everyone had to wait until the court decided what would happen. The court divided everything equally between the two sons. The house had to be sold so each would get half of its worth. The two sons and their families are angry at each other, and they have stopped speaking to each other.

♣ **food for thought**

There is real beauty to be found in knowing that your end is going to catch up with you faster than you expected, and that you have to get all your living and laughing and crying done as soon as you can.

— Lyn Helton

A legal will lets you decide about these things:

- Who will care of the children if their mother and father are no longer alive? This person is called a *guardian*.

- Who will have your things after you die?

- Who will make sure your wishes are followed after you die? This person is called an *executor*.

Good reasons to have a will

- If you do not have a will, the court will make these decisions for you.

- A will gets things settled quickly for everyone—much more quickly than waiting for the courts to name an *administrator* to look after things.

You can hire a lawyer to write a will, or you can write what you want on a piece of paper. Sometimes families won't accept these handwritten wills, so the whole thing has to go to court. This can take a lot of time. This is why

it's safer to get a lawyer's help. Your family and friends will have peace of mind if they don't have to guess or argue over what they think you wanted.

You will need to sign and date your will. You will also need two witnesses to sign it in front of you. They must be over 19 years old, and they must be people who are not getting anything in the will.

Here are things that can go in a legal will and things that can go in a letter.

Some things to put in a legal will

- People who receive property or money

- A list of your favourite things and whom you want to give them to

- The name of the Guardian for your children

- The Executor who will make sure your wishes are followed

- How your debts are to be paid

Some things to put in a letter

- Your plans for your funeral or service

- Your plans about donating your organs

- Your Spiritual Will

Living Will

A Living Will is something you might want to write when you are able to make decisions about yourself. A Living Will is also called an *advance directive* or a *personal directive*. This kind of will tells health-care workers what kind of medical treatment you want if you cannot make decisions for yourself. Sometimes accident or a serious illness can cause us to be unconscious or not be mentally able to make important decisions about our health care.

❧ food for thought
Do not follow where the path may lead. Go instead where there is no path and leave a trail.

— Raph Waldo Emerson

Here is an example of how a Living Will works. You might be in the hospital dying of cancer. If you stop breathing, do you want doctors to try to restart your heart or not? If you do not want doctors to restart you heart, you would put "Do not resuscitate" (DNR) in your Living Will.

Before you make a Living Will, talk to a doctor about what medical choices might lie ahead. Then write your Living Will making these things clear:

- Which treatments you want and don't want.
- Whether or not you want doctors to do everything possible to keep you alive.
- If you want to donate your organs after death.
- Who will make sure your Living Will is honoured.

You can write the Living Will or ask someone to write it for you. Be sure to sign it in front of a witness. Then, ask the witness to sign it too. Give a copy of your Living Will to someone who will make sure your wishes are carried out. It's a good idea to also give a copy to your lawyer. Each province, territory, and state has different ways of naming and handling Living Wills.

Spiritual Will

A Spiritual Will is a loving gift you leave to your children, family, and friends. You have lived a life full of experiences and learning. A Spiritual Will is a way to share your love with those you will be leaving behind. It is a time for you to tell your stories.

❖ **food for thought**

Let your life lightly dance on the edges of Time like dew on the tip of a leaf.

— Tagore

Here are some suggestions for what you might put in a Spiritual Will:

> **A life map.** You can draw a river or a tree and write in special events or times in your life. For example, at the beginning of the river or at the roots of the tree, write the date you were born. Then move along the river or up the trunk of the tree, and write down other big moments in your life. There is no right or wrong way to do this. Follow your heart.
>
> **Your stories.** Think of the stories you want to share— challenges or adventures or funny events. These can teach important life lessons you want others to know. They might be bits of wisdom you have gathered, or funny stories that tell others more about you. You can write these down or talk into a tape recorder, or tell someone else who can write or type for you.
>
> **Hopes for the future.** Say what you hope for each person in your family as well as for your friends, your community, and even the world.
>
> **Things your grandfather or grandmother taught you.** Your family would be grateful to hear stories about your parents and grandparents that only you know.

♣ **food for thought**

I wanted a perfect ending. Now I've learned, the **hard** way, that **some poems don't** rhyme, and some stories don't have a clear beginning, middle, and end. Life is about not knowing, having to change, taking the moment and making the best of it, without knowing what's going to happen next.

— Gilda Radner

Make sure someone close to you knows where your Spiritual Will can be found after your die.

Planning Your Service

If you want a funeral or memorial service, here are some questions to think about. Before you decide, talk it over with someone. Then write down your wishes and give them to someone close to you.

What kind of service do you want?
Write your ideas in the boxes on the right.

Decisions	What I want...
○ Do I want to be buried in a casket or do I want to be cremated?	
○ Do I want family and friends to be able to see my body after death or do I want a closed casket?	
○ Where do I want to be buried?	

Decisions	What I want…

○ If I am cremated, what do I want done with the ashes?
   • buried in an urn
   • kept by people I care about
   • scattered in a special place	

○ Do I want a traditional service in a church, mosque, synagogue or do I want a service in my home or outdoors in nature?	
○ Who should lead the service?	
○ Do I want some photos displayed? If so, which ones?	
○ Do I want some readings at my service? If so, which ones? Who should read them?	
○ Do I want music? What kind? Do I want someone to play or sing?	

Decisions	What I want...
○ Do I want a notice in the newspaper? Who should write it? What do I want them to say?	
○ Do I want flowers? If so, what kind?	
○ Do I want people to give money to a charity? If so, which one?	
○ Do I want lots of people at my service or a few special ones?	
○ Is there anything else I'd like, such as a tree planted in my memory?	
○ What helps me when I have to face challenges? For example, I talk about it with a friend.	
○ How can I make this a meaningful time for me and my loved ones?	

In beauty may I walk.

All day long may I walk.

Through the returning seasons may I walk.

On the trail marked with pollen may I walk.

With grasshoppers about my feet may I walk.

With dew about my feet may I walk.

With beauty may I walk.

With beauty before me may I walk.

With beauty behind me may I walk.

With beauty above me, may I walk.

With beauty below me, may I walk.

With beauty all around me, may I walk.

In old age wandering on a trail of beauty, lively, may I walk.

It is finished in beauty.

It is finished in beauty.

— A Navajo Indian Prayer

Before you make your final choices, ask a funeral director about costs. Tell them up front how much you can spend and they will help you decide what you can afford. They might also suggest ideas where you can get some financial help. If your funeral costs will be more than you can afford, talk with a financial worker at social services.

Dying or thinking about dying is a sad time for you and everyone close to you. Try to do all you can to prepare for that time, and you will feel more peaceful. You will know that your family and friends will be looked after in the best way. You will then have more time to think about how you want to live the life you have left. ●

❖ **food for thought**

Farm as if you would live forever, and live as if you would die tomorrow.

— George Henderson

References and Credits

References

1 Noel, B., and Blair, P.D. PhD. (2000). *I wasn't ready to say goodbye.* Milwaukee, WI: Champion Press, Ltd. pp. 55-56. Reprinted with permission.

2 Gould, J. (1997). *Answering children's questions about death: A guide for children and adults.* Los Angeles, CA: Hillside Memorial Park and Mortuary.

3 Poetseers. Sri Chinmoy Centre. Retrieved September 8, 2006 from http://www.poetseers.org/contemporary_poets/mary/